Around the World with Queen Mylan

Mylan A. J. Morisseau

Sula Too Publishing
www.sulatoo.com/publishing

Around the World with Queen Mylan

Copyright © 2022 Mylan A. J. Morisseau
All rights reserved. No part of this book may be reproduced, stored, or transmitted by any means whether auditory, graphic, mechanical, or electronic without written permission of both publisher and author, except in the case of brief excerpts used in critical articles and reviews. Unauthorized reproduction of any part of this work is illegal and is punishable by law.

Cover Design by Tonya Mills
First Printing by The Alhaven Group Publishing

Printed in the United States of America
ISBN: 979-8-9865280-1-4 Hard cover
Published by Sula Too Publishing
Tampa, Florida
www.sulatoo.com/publishing

Special Acknowledgments

I am incredibly grateful to have the following people in my life that believed in me and encouraged me to complete this special project.

I am truly thankful for my mother, Dr. Mavis Morisseau for her unwavering support and patience with me during this journey. She provides tremendous motivation to me and she is my biggest cheerleader. Love you, dearly!

A heartfelt thanks to my beautiful family and friends, Joseph Rollins Jr. and Family, Dr. Kai Dupé, Orr Family, Givens Family, Banks Family, Cyrs Family, Bain Family, Brittany M. Allen, Phyllis Jordan, Janice Suitte, and Karyle Thornton. You all believed in my gifts and I am now able to see it to its fruition. Much Love!

I would also like to acknowledge Dr. Mateen A. Diop, my Uncle and Ms. Tonya Mills, Illustrator. Your wonderful contributions, dedication, and time are very much appreciated!

Welcome to the AMAZING world with Queen Mylan.

A world of adventure, culture, love, and fun. Sit back and relax as we go for a ride; a ride that will open your eyes to new horizons and undiscovered treasures. So get ready everybody as we fly away from Miami, Florida to travel the world and enjoy it's many hidden treasures.

Fly Adwoa Javeen Airways!

Royal Family, let's get ready to go on an amazing journey!

King Josiah, Queen Akosua, Princess Hadassa, Princess Yasmeen, & Princess Payton

Grab your passports, tickets, and luggage!

It's time to take a trip with Queen Mylan!

The Places We Will Visit!

Can you locate the different places we will visit during our journey?

- ☐ Grand Canyon National Park, Arizona
- ☐ Seattle/Tacoma, Washington
- ☐ Ontario, Canada
- ☐ Anchorage, Alaska
- ☐ Panaluu, Hawaii
- ☐ Melbourne, Australia
- ☐ Jakarta, Indonesia
- ☐ Manila, Philippines
- ☐ Okinawa, Japan
- ☐ Seoul, South Korea
- ☐ Southeast Asia
- ☐ Prague, Czech Republic
- ☐ Dubrovnik, Croatia
- ☐ Huralwaldi, Maldives
- ☐ Dubai, United Arab Emirates
- ☐ Milan, Italy
- ☐ Pamukkale, Turkey
- ☐ Paris, France
- ☐ Brussels, Belgium
- ☐ Fairy Pools, Isle of Skye, Scotland
- ☐ Timbuktu, Mali
- ☐ Ghana
- ☐ Cameroon
- ☐ Cairo, Egypt
- ☐ Uganda
- ☐ Kenya
- ☐ Tanzania
- ☐ Madagascar
- ☐ Port au Prince, Haiti
- ☐ Costa Rica
- ☐ Panama City, Panama
- ☐ São Paulo, Brazil
- ☐ Buenos Aires, Argentina
- ☐ Libya
- ☐ Ethiopia

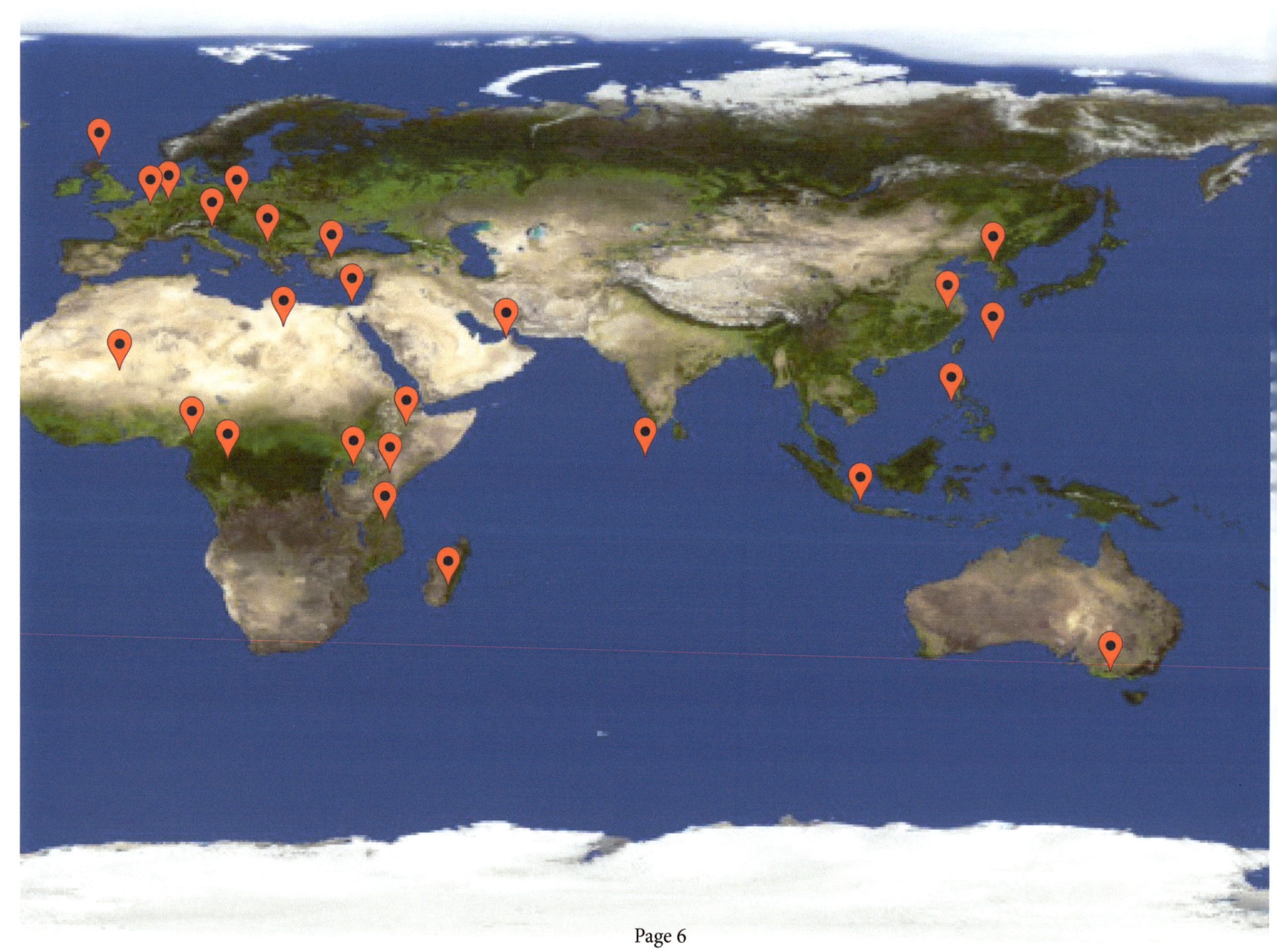

Hello Kiddos!

Now I know everyone is excited for school, but today we shall be going on a different kind of adventure. This means we won't be in a classroom of four walls today, but instead we will be making the world our classroom. So, who's ready for the adventure to begin? The plane is right outside.

Grand Canyon National Park, Arizona

Hey kids, look out your windows because what you will find down below is rocky terrain with rivers and streams. And just like in class we will learn about the indigenous and sedimentary.

So, gather your samples, because we just might make a scientific discovery.

Fun Facts: To view the Grand Canyon people take helicopter rides into the canyon.

 # Seattle/Tacoma, Washington

OK girls and boys we have made it to the home of the space needle. I hear the view from the top of the needle is an extraordinary sight to see. Soo, lets land the plane and climb to the top to and have a quick munch on croissants from the original Starbucks.

Then we must be off for our international expedition.

Fun Facts: Edward E. Carlson doodled an idea of a dominant central structure for the World's Fair on a napkin in a hotel café. That central structure became known as the Space Needle.

Ontario, Canada

Kids? Guess what? We are going to see our first castle. Then we will visit Niagara Falls and if we have time we just might get to conquer the Rocky's.

We can ski down slopes and sip hot chocolate. And just before it's time to go we'll make snow angels and sing carols.

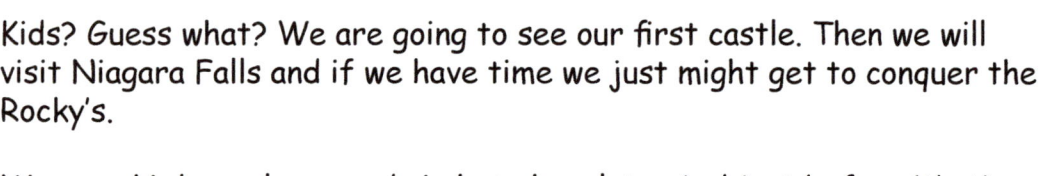

Fun Facts: There are two sides to Niagara Falls. One southern side is in the United States. The northern side is in Ontario, Canada.

Anchorage, Alaska

OK Kids, it's time to put on your coats and hop in some boats. Here in a Alaska we will go ice fishing and star gazing. And if we're lucky we just might see the dancing lights as we grab a quick bite. Anyways it's time to take flight.

Fun Facts: Alaska has the longest and shortest day on the planet. The longest day last three months and the longest night last two months.

Punaluu, Hawaii

Well, my little conquerors we have now entered one of mother nature's most beautiful and interesting creations ... BLACK SAND BEACHES. And this extravagant place is called Punaluu (PU- NA- LUU).
Isn't it a charming sight to see? Let's go run through the sand and make sand angels...We will have a grand time before we have to take to the skies, There will be many more sights to see. So, let's hurry.

Fun Facts: Hawaii is the only state in the USA to have two official languages, Hawaiian and English.

Melbourne, Australia

Now, I know we love marine-life, but have you ever seen glowing water? In the mystical land of
Australia, there are bio-luminescent (bio-lum-in-nes- cent) waves. Some think the water is glowing, but the water is just filled with glowing jellyfish. It must be an amazing site to see at night when the beaches light up and the waves are peaceful.

The marine-life in Australia is just one of the many things that make it such a mystical place. The natives of the land also bring magic to this land.

The natives are called Aboriginal Australians.

These natives are known for living in the Bush of Australia (not just a single bush, silly); these people are amazing trackers and hunters. Although, the people don't have much, they sure do have a lot of love and history to give, even in the down under.

Fun Facts: Australia is both a country and a continent.

📍 Jakarta, Indonesia

Hey kids, open your eyes. We have made it to our next destination. The sun is rising and shining on the sands of INDONESIA. WOAH! Did you feel that rumbling? That rumbling was the active volcanoes on this exuberant island.

Now, follow me kids as we explore the island and its treasures.

We can run through the Jatiluwih rice fields and then go swimming in Lake Toba. And before we return to our flight we will hug the natives goodbye.

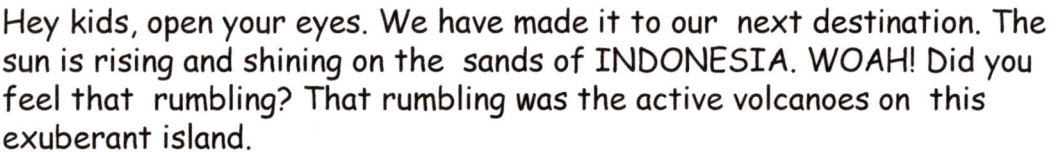

Fun Facts: 100 out of the 400 volcanoes in Indonesia are active.

Page 14

Manila, Philippines

Look kiddos as we cross over the valleys, oceans, and seas, we are traveling northeast towards the Philippines. You see, the caves are deep and the river runs into the sea.

Now, let us hop out this plane and into a boat, so that we can travel into the underground cove. The Puerto Princesa River is a cave filled with its own special water. And after the tour we will have to take flight for their are more adventures to come.

Fun Facts: The Philippines is the world's largest exporter of coconuts and other tropical fruit like, papaya.

Okinawa, Japan

Well kids who wants to say a funny word with me? I don't want to say it by myself, so are you ready? (OKEY- NA-WA) Let's go slow as we go through OKINAWA, Japan. It is a magical land filled with vibrant colors and music. A place filled with cherry blossom gardens and magical caves.

We can explore the land right now, while Pilot Akousa refuels the plane for our nighttime adventure.

Fun Facts: Okinawa is the fifth largest island of Japan's 6,852 islands. Out of the 6,000 plus islands, only 421 are inhabited.

Seoul, South Korea

This night-time adventure has only begun. We still have rainbows, rivers, forests, and more of mother nature's beautiful and magical creations to see. Buuuuuuutttt for now, we will be stopping in South Korea to behold rainbows at night.
Banpo Bridge is a sight to see at night; close your eyes and run with me.

Run with me kids, run until we dash over the rainbow and maybe just maybe, we will find a pot of gold.

Fun Facts: South Koreans will usually be older than someone of their same age, because they count themselves as one year old at birth.

Southeast Asia

As much as we love South Korea, I have a more magical and peculiar land. This wonderful place is found in Southeast Asia. The people there do not live on land, but on the seas. So, let's dive deep into the culture and life of the Bajau Laut people.

Did you know that they live in the most peculiar of ways? They do not wish to live on land for they enjoy life on the seas. They hunt for their own food and they make a living off what they catch and sell. And not to mention, They are brilliant people and are excellent swimmers, too. It almost makes me wish I could hold my breath for 13 minutes too. Do you wish that you could hold your breath underwater for that long?

Fun Facts: This region is popular for tourism because of it's tropical climate, which causes it to be warm throughout the year.

# Prague, Czech Republic

Czech Republic is where we have landed. I thought we might go through the market and meet new people. Then, we can go to Prague and explore the many castles and gardens that are over hundreds of years old. The richness of this land is truly beautiful and refreshing, kids.

Take in the view with me, before we take to the skies again.

Fun Facts: In Europe, you will find most castles located in Czech Republic.

Dubrovnik, Croatia

It's almost dark and before our night-time adventure begins, we have one more stop in the land of Croatia. Have you ever wanted to jump off waterfalls and run along trails that lead to beautiful sights? Well then, this is the place to be. The water is a vivid turquoise and the forest surrounding it is thick and full of life.

Sounds like the place to be for some beautiful photography, nature walks, swimming, and maybe even some creativity for all my little artists, don't you think?

Fun Facts: The Tesla car, is named after the Croatian inventor Nikola Tesla, who had over 270 inventions.

Huralwaldi, Maldives

OK kiddos we are now landing in one of the world's smallest countries. The Maldives have a very rich marine life, but there are only a few land animals. The coral reefs and sea animals are plentiful. In the Maldives we shall snorkel among sea turtles.

Then we will feed flying foxes and fruit bats, and some reptiles such as geckos, lizards and non- poisonous snakes. And after all is said and done we will take to the skies again.

Fun Facts: Dogs are not allowed on the Maldives.

# Dubai, United Arab Emirates

Well now, I think it's time that we get sandy again in the uniqueness of Dubai. Do you know what a sandstorm is? Well, for all our new-comers, a sandstorm is like a thick cloud of sand and wind that covers the land from time to time.

If you like getting dirty just stay outside in the storm and when it's time to wash off, you will be scrubbing dust and sand off you for hours. It is time we get back on the plane; I think a storm is coming soo... TAKE COVER!!!

Fun Facts: Dubai has no street addresses, everything is delivered to a PO boxes. In Dubai you can find the world's tallest building of 164 floors.

Milan, Italy

Well then kiddos i think it's time to switch it up. Do you like fashion? I know I like fashion. Our current stop is in Milan, Italy, where fashion is booming.

Milan is known as the money-making heart of Italy. Fun fact, my name is Mylan. And just like you and I are works of art made by the best artist, Milan has some of the best artists and works of art known to man. Would you like to see? Look closely, I think we are about to meet the great Da Vinci.

Fun Facts: The Milan Cathedral took more than 555 years to build and about 5 million people go to visit the Cathedral yearly.

Pamukkale, Turkey

Come on kids let's go bathe in the hot spring city of Pamukkale. We have officially landed in Turkey, so we might as well go for a dip.

The thermal springs were also used as a healing center by doctors during Cleopatra's time as Queen. So swimming where a queen once swam should make us also feel like royalty. Well before we take flight we might have to stop and find ourselves some crowns.

Fun Facts: All visitors can bathe in the Hot Springs no plumbing needed..

 Paris, France

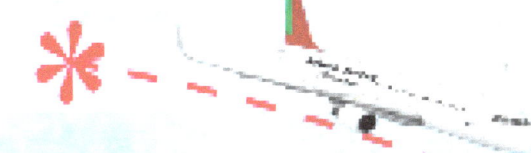

Kids, pay attention as we fly high over the Eiffel Tower. And maybe we will land right outside Disneyland, if we ask Pilot Akousa nicely.

And before we hop back on the plane we will stop in a bakery and get some crepes with whip cream.

Fun Facts: For four decades the Eiffel Tower, was the world's tallest
structure and it was once yellow.

Brussels, Belgium

Ok, come on now my little adventurers. We have landed in the cool rainy lands of Belgium, but we are specifically in Brussels. We have only stopped here for a snack, so what do you think we should try?
Do we want pastries for the flight or do we want sausage and waffles?

The waffles will melt in your mouth and the sausage will taste like sweet maple. Not to mention, the pastries will hit that sweet spot like a home run.
Don't forget to sample the ice cream from the world famous, Häagen Dazs. Now, hurry upland and get your snack kids, we will soon have to take to the skies again.

Fun Facts: Belgium is the world's largest exporter of chocolate. In Belgium they produce 220,000 tons of chocolate annually.

# Fairy Pools, Isle of Skye, Scotland

Have you ever seen a fairy? I guess it's time you learn about fairies as our next stop will be Scotland. There are these pools in Scotland, called The Fairy Pools, Isle of Skye. Legend has it that a great chief long ago married a fairy princess and that is how the pools got their names.

But, did you know that you can also see the northern lights in Scotland? I bet that would be a sight to see on a cool summer night. Anyways to the plane we go as we take flight we will see the many dancing lights.

Fun Facts: Isle of Skye is a magnificent island with many different breeds of sheep. Here, sheep outnumber humans 10:1.

Timbuktu, Mali

Wow! Look where we are landing now, in the magical land of TIMBUKTU. A place with beautiful pyramids and castles.

There is only sand as far as the eye can see. And I bet you are wondering why there is so much sand around; It is because this magical land is perched on the edge of the Saharan desert.

Fun Facts: Timbuktu is a word commonly used to express that a location is far away.

Ghana

Who's ready for lunch? Let's go eat something nice! Since ancient times here, Ghana has given out the best salts and spices!

If your fridge ever runs warm or doesn't have ice, the people can teach you a secret once or twice! And before we take flight we must remember to collect some spice.

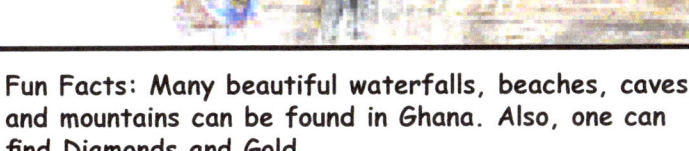

Fun Facts: Many beautiful waterfalls, beaches, caves, and mountains can be found in Ghana. Also, one can find Diamonds and Gold.

Cameroon

For our next destination on this trip, we will land our plane near Mt. Cameroon, the active volcano that stands tall above the seas. We can collect little trinkets in the village and then we can visit the Blackitude Museum and learn about the heritage.
Then, we shall be off to the Ekom-Nkam waterfalls and the Limbe Botanic Garden.

There is so much beauty in this blessed land and I wish we had more time to explore it all, but it is time for our next adventure.

Fun Facts: Cameroon has 220,000 sq km of tropical forests which is home to 900 bird species and over 300 mammals.

Page 30

Cairo, Egypt

Come on kids, the plane has now landed in the terrain of the pyramids. This is the motherland of kings and queens who ruled the plains of Egypt. From hidden tombs to the magnificent Sphinx, this is a land full of treasure and life.

From the Nile river to the desert sands, there is life. Now kids, who wants to catch frogs with me in the Nile?

Fun Facts: The Nile river runs through or along the border of 11 African countries. The Nile river greatly supported the development of ancient Egypt.

 # Uganda

Ok kids, our adventure is almost over, but first we must stop in the land of Uganda. We are off to visit tribes of every kind. We are here to play and dance and help plant in the motherland's soil.

There is a lot of fun to be had in this fruitful land. Are you ready to meet chiefs and priests and learn about the different cultures that rule this terrain?

Fun Facts: In Uganda there are over 50 different tribes. The different cultures can be seen through the food, music, language, and dress.

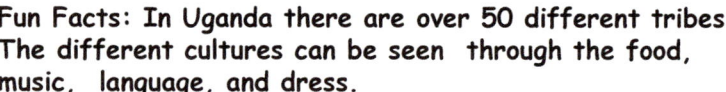

 Kenya

Okay team, we are going to see a race! We will root for Kenya, because they will win first place! The runners will keep us up to pace. Make sure to first tie your shoelace!

On your mark, get set, GO!

Fun Facts: In Kenya, you can find cheetahs, the fastest moving land animal in the world.

Tanzania

We are going from Kenya to Tanzania, oh the beauty we will see!
I have an idea to share. Let us travel from the mountains to the vast plains, where the mass Safari lives within this African domain. The lions will shake their manes, and we will taste sweet food from the sugarcanes.

Fun Facts: Located in Tanzania, Mount Kilimanjaro is the highest free-standing mountain in the world. (It is not apart of a mountain range.)

Madagascar

Come on kiddos, let's hop off this plane for another adventure. We have landed in the beautiful terrain of Madagascar. A home to many different species of animals, but specifically lemurs and chameleons that run wild in this beautiful land. Did you know that Madagascar is also the fourth biggest island in the world?

Before we end our visit, we could take a dip in the cool blue waters that surround this beautiful place. Wow, that was fun, we now have to hop on a plane to our next destination.

Fun Facts: There are many exotic animals in Madagascar, but you will not find some animals there such as tigers or giraffes.

Port au Prince, Haiti

Ok, my little conquerors we are now landing in Port au Prince, Haiti. It is a beautiful Caribbean island nation on the Hispaniola with the Dominican Republic lying to its east. It's rich history and cultural depth have shaped the country into what it is today. Filled with misty mountain tops, golden beaches and turquoise blue water.

Haiti is also known for their mangos, so before we take flight again we should gather mangos to take home.

Fun Facts: Haiti means the land of mountains.

Costa Rica

Well kiddos, since we are island hopping I think it is time we land in Costa Rica. When we land the first thing we shall do is visit the waterfalls. We may also run into some wildlife while on our adventure. And if we are in search of treasure then treasure we shall find in a land of rich beauty and life.

Also before we take flight again we will meet some natives and learn some history.

Fun Facts: Whale Beach (Costa Ballina) is shaped like a whale tail ! How exciting!

Panama City, Panama

Republic of Panama is where our amazing pilot has landed us. Panama is the country that joins Central America to South America. Anyways we are going to be traveling through the jungles to meet some big cats.

We will play with cubs and we will hop on boats and travel down streams. And when all is said and done we will take to the skies again.

Fun Facts: Panama's rainforests are home to 5 species of big cats: pumas, jaguars, jaguarundis, margays and ocelots.

São Paulo, Brazil

OK kids! Repeat after me, "North America, South America, Africa... HEY! Why' did you stop?
Do you already know where we are? South America?
Well, aren't you all just a bunch of smarties. Do you know where we are exactly? We are in Brazil. Brazil is known for the Amazon which we will talk about in our wildlife adventures.

Brazil is also known for its energetic culture, fun dances, exciting martial arts, and beautiful sceneries.

Fun Facts: Brazil is a very colorful place. It is the largest country in South America and home of over 211 million people.

 # Buenos Aires, Argentina

Where to next? Our next night time stop is Buenos Aires, Argentina. We are currently visiting the mesmerizing sculpture, Floralis Genérica.

Can you guess what this sculpture is made out of? I hope you guessed metal. It almost looks like a huge mirror, doesn't it? Do you know you can see the city's reflection in this sculpture? You can also see just how beautiful and bright the city is, even at night while the stars line the skies.

Fun Facts: The world's widest street is located in Buenos Aires. This street is called "Avenida 9 de Julio" and it is 12 lanes wide.

 Libya

This is our next to last adventure, kiddos. I don't know if I can say goodbye...maybe. I am going to hate to say farewell, because our adventures will be ending soon. So, who is ready to explore this ancient land of the Romans and Greeks?

I see that you are ready to dance on the sandy Saharan desert or skip in the cool waves of the Benghazi Beach. Another thing to do is play hide and seek in the ruins of the ancient ones. It was so refreshing to visit here. Onto the next adventure!

Fun Facts: The Libyan Desert is known for going decades without rain.

Adwoa Javeen International Resort, Ethiopia

Hey kids, wake up. We have landed in Ethiopia. This is the ADWOA JAVEEN INTERNATIONAL RESORT.

I know after the constant changes in time zones you will want to sleep in another nice comfy bed fit for the princesses that you are. Go ahead and take that nap, because when you wake up, we will have a nice breakfast prepared for you. Later, you guys can swim in the pool, or play in the indoor park, and if we have time, we will stop in lego-land to top off the fun.

Now we are off to the Fine Arts Academy where Princesses Paityn, Laila, and Hadassa await to teach us words in Swahili and the meaning of the celebration to come as well as the meaning of faith, family and unity.

Fun Facts: Coffee grown worldwide can trace it origins back to Ethiopia.

Adwoa Javeen Vegetarian Cuisine Restaurant

Hey kids, we have a super duper adventure, it's so cool seeing all of the new things and meeting new friends.

We are hungry now! Let's go eat!

TODAY'S MENU

MAIN MEAL:
   BROWN RICE   AVOCADO
   BLACK BEANS
   LENTIL POTATO NUGGETS
   VEGGIE PIZZA

DESERTS:
   RICE CAKES
   JELLO

TO DRINK:
   LEMONGRASS TEA

Adwoa Javeen Fine Arts and Music Academy

Hey kids, we have finally arrived at the school. I think it is about time we get ready for the celebration. We have flyers and banners and goodies to make. A few things to learn and a lot of games to play. If we have time, we might just get a little messy with finger paints and glue.

This celebration of Black History is a time to learn and a time to share, a time to reflect and a time to care; so before Prince Michael James, Zion, and Prince Alexander return with their toys and genuine joy, we must be ready to welcome Princesses Yasmeen, Payton, Victoria, Caroleena, Angelina, Aliyah, Paityn, and Lailah, with open arms and gifts in our hands. This is the celebration where family will grow closer and our creativity will soar. So, open your minds to all the possibilities and more.

BLACK HISTORY CELEBRATION!
HONORING BLACK HISTORY

What a beautiful time of celebration all year around!!
Let's look at these **Leaders**, **Legends**, and **Legacies**!!

Look at our lineage and our heritage! These are the shoulders that we stand on every day!

Martin Luther King, Jr.	Mansa Musa	Malcolm X.
Dr. Benjamin E. Mays		Marcus Garvey
Daniel Hale Williams		Maya Angelou
Althea Gibson		Ruby Bridges
Arthuro Schomburg		Ronald McNair
Fred Jones		Bessie Coleman
Mae C. Jemison		Rebecca Lee Crumpler
Ron Finley		Henry Ossian Flipper Claudette Colvin
Matthew Henson		Alice Alison Dunnigan
Toussaint Louverture		Septima Poinsette Clark Charles Leclerc
Jean Jacques Dessalines		Alexandre
Henry Cristophe		

BLACK HISTORY CELEBRATION!
OUR FUTURE LEADERS & TRAILBLAZERS

Here are some amazing young leaders from our future generations.
Let's gleam from them.

Prince	Princess	Princess	Princess	Princess	Princess
Prince	Prince	Princess	Queen	Princess	King

Farewell!!

Now that the adventure is done and it is time to run, we will fly away to meet your loved ones. Do not forget to teach them all you have learned. I would like you to remember that just because after our final destination it doesn't mean that the adventure has to end.

I will return again with more surprises and spectacular fun. So, as we say farewell, I will leave you with a clue for our next adventure.

Dark as night and cool as ice,
the sirens call and the pirate's gold.
far away and down below,
a world of life we have yet to know.
Follow me to where the creatures glow and the kingdom of the unknown awaits.
Where are we going next???

About the Illustrator

Ms. Tonya Mills has worked in education for over 25 years and loves to be creative with digital art and illustrations. Her book designs include, 'Created by God, so we must be special" by Dr. Mavis Morisseau. Tonya has a gift and passion for designing book covers, custom logos, posters, and badges.

Photo Citations from Images sourced from Pixabay and other sites:

https://pixabay.com/photos/purple-background-grunge-texture-608575/ | https://pixabay.com/photos/manchester-airport-england-1555612/ | https://pixabay.com/photos/aviator-begin-take-off-lift-up-1359867/ | https://pixabay.com/vectors/passport-ticket-travel-entry-159592/ | https://pixabay.com/photos/aurora-polar-lights-northern-lights-1185464/ | https://pixabay.com/photos/polar-bear-bear-sea-bear-white-404314/ | https://pixabay.com/photos/grey-seal-helgoland-dune-sand-3281160/ | https://pixabay.com/photos/black-sand-beach-hawaii-maui-91666/ |https://pixabay.com/photos/beach-secret-fantasy-surreal-4025389/ | https://pixabay.com/photos/tribal-natives-tradition-culture-262471/ |https://pixabay.com/photos/national-park-australia-aboriginal-2054925/ | https://pixabay.com/photos/bali-indonesia-paddy-fields-harvest-2394490/ | https://pixabay.com/photos/indonesia-mountain-cloud-volcano-5008886/ | https://pixabay.com/photos/beach-sea-stone-water-blue-cave-3959845/ | https://pixabay.com/photos/coconut-fruit-tropical-fruit-bud-4644549/ | https://pixabay.com/photos/cherry-blossoms-landscape-spring-2218781/ |https://pixabay.com/photos/map-globe-countries-3476649/ | https://pixabay.com/photos/korean-folk-village-forest-trees-5286449/ | https://pixabay.com/photos/korea-incheon-ganghwado-landscape-2832422/ | https://pixabay.com/photos/huts-sea-moorea-lagoon-beach-5790006/ | https://pixabay.com/photos/prague-praha-winter-night-3010407/ |https://pixabay.com/photos/castle-palace-building-architecture-5588005/ | https://pixabay.com/photos/hluboka-castle-castle-architecture-6475830/ | https://pixabay.com/photos/krka-waterfall-croatia-nature-park-987021/ | https://pixabay.com/photos/lake-blue-forest-plitvice-croatia-476792/ | https://pixabay.com/photos/sea-sunset-romantic-dubai-3496528/ | https://pixabay.com/photos/burj-khalifa-building-dubai-city-1096446/ | https://pixabay.com/photos/italy-duomo-square-milan-3523720/ | https://pixabay.com/photos/italy-milano-duomo-square-3523635/ | https://pixabay.com/photos/leonardo-da-vinci-sculpture-statue-3526516/ | https://pixabay.com/photos/brugge-bruges-belgium-architecture-5278796/ | https://pixabay.com/photos/belgium-waffle-flag-1279842/ | https://pixabay.com/photos/aurora-borealis-northern-lights-2647474/ | https://pixabay.com/photos/stirling-castle-scotland-stirling-202103/ | https://pixabay.com/photos/ireland-sheep-lambs-livestock-1985088/ | https://pixabay.com/photos/desert-sand-dunes-landscape-1654439/ | https://pixabay.com/photos/desert-landscapes-sahara-4933581/ | https://pixabay.com/photos/camel-wadi-rum-desert-travel-1120371/ | https://pixabay.com/photos/ghana-africa-village-life-1809404/ | https://pixabay.com/photos/ghana-africa-cocoa-culture-country-2842927 | https://pixabay.com/photos/ghana-boy-child-grinning-cute-80832/ | https://pixabay.com/photos/mount-cameroon-africa-1489500/ | https://pixabay.com/photos/mount-cameroon-africa-1489500/ | https://pixabay.com/photos/child-smile-africa-cameroon-3836310/ | https://pixabay.com/photos/sphinx-pyramids-historic-egypt-350458/ | https://pixabay.com/photos/river-nile-egypt-sailboat-dhow-378495/ | https://pixabay.com/photos/rocks-river-falls-murchison-falls-6351404/ | https://pixabay.com/photos/chief-cameroon-africa-1645196/ | https://pixabay.com/photos/tourism-uganda-karamoja-4169709/ | https://pixabay.com/photos/mount-kilimanjaro-mountain-safari-1025146/ | https://pixabay.com/photos/people-man-guy-running-sport-2590796/ | https://pixabay.com/photos/people-group-many-child-education-3137672/ | https://pixabay.com/photos/lion-cub-cat-wild-wild-cat-565820/ | https://pixabay.com/photos/kilimanjaro-tanzania-africa-4436821/ | https://pixabay.com/photos/madagascar-baobabs-tree-baobab-4587230/ | https://pixabay.com/photos/madagascar-africa-women-island-see-4601287/ | https://pixabay.com/photos/lemur-curious-halfaap-peek-a-boo-3295891/ | https://pixabay.com/photos/brazil-rio-landscape-tourism-ocean-4809014/ | https://pixabay.com/photos/portrait-northeast-culture-4381900/ | https://pixabay.com/photos/floralis-generica-buenos-aires-6587192/ | https://pixabay.com/photos/sea-of-silver-argentina-buenos-aires-2206214/ | https://pixabay.com/photos/oasis-libya-lake-quiet-reflection-1997849/ | https://pixabay.com/photos/libya-tuareg-hookah-2284276/ | https://pixabay.com/photos/tripoli-libya-city-africa-capital-2229019/ | https://pixabay.com/photos/hotel-cuba-leisure-resort-vacation-1111199/ | https://pixabay.com/photos/gallaudet-university-schools-1607734/ | https://pixabay.com/vectors/candleholder-candle-holder-152035/ | https://pixabay.com/photos/tavern-crete-sea-vacations-1362960/ | https://pixabay.com/photos/woman-teacher-model-board-5462074/ | https://pixabay.com/vectors/camera-lens-photography-32871/ | https://pixabay.com/vectors/lion-animal-head-feline-big-cat-6471831/ | https://www.vecteezy.com/free-vector/african-print, African Print Vectors by Vecteezy | https://pixabay.com/vectors/africa-continent-geography-map-151585/#comments | https://pixabay.com/vectors/woman-colorful-people-africa-158343/ | https://pixabay.com/photos/air-new-zealand-airplanes-airport-5669414/ | https://pixabay.com/photos/grand-canyon-landscape-park-nature-1083745/ | https://pixabay.com/photos/grand-canyon-america-desert-2159269/ | https://pixabay.com/photos/seattle-space-needle-skyline-6093144/ | https://pixabay.com/photos/city-skyscrapers-seattle-sunset-5985491/ | https://pixabay.com/photos/hot-air-balloons-adventure-balloons-1867279/ | https://pixabay.com/photos/waters-nature-lake-heaven-3168662/ | https://pixabay.com/photos/children-ski-lessons-exercise-hills-3167588/ | https://pixabay.com/photos/beach-resort-jetty-pier-boardwalk-666122/ | https://pixabay.com/photos/maldives-trip-color-underwater-1268661/ | https://pixabay.com/photos/atoll-beach-couple-destination-2179102/ | https://pixabay.com/photos/pamukkale-turquoise-14977/ | https://pixabay.com/photos/pamukkale-hierapolis-turkey-ancient-4917193/ | https://pixabay.com/photos/pamukkale-column-antique-423481/ | https://pixabay.com/photos/paris-france-eiffel-eiffel-tower-1175022/ | https://pixabay.com/photos/eiffel-tower-france-paris-landscape-975004/ | https://pixabay.com/photos/notre-dame-paris-cathedral-france-503866/ | https://pixabay.com/photos/building-architecture-landmark-102840/ | https://pixabay.com/photos/amphitheater-theatre-stage-5383436/ | https://pixabay.com/photos/arc-de-triomphe-paris-landmark-5432392/ | https://pixabay.com/photos/labadee-haiti-royal-caribbean-1167166/ | https://pixabay.com/photos/children-haiti-carrefour-2704878/ | https://pixabay.com/photos/crabs-haiti-shellfish-seafood-2422026/ | https://pixabay.com/photos/beach-sunset-coast-costa-rica-2580656/ | https://pixabay.com/photos/scarlet-macaw-tropical-bird-3924046/ | https://pixabay.com/photos/volcano-costa-rica-clouds-blue-sky-2355772/ | https://pixabay.com/photos/panama-city-ocean-nature-4198941/ | https://pixabay.com/photos/panama-panama-city-the-panama-canal-4948005/ | https://pixabay.com/photos/rain-forest-palm-trees-river-273780/ | https://pixabay.com/photos/panama-sloth-child-mother-family-3638527/ | https://pixabay.com/photos/puma-wildcat-predator-animal-4190562/ | https://pixabay.com/photos/pumpkins-fall-multicoloured-october-4586250/ | https://pixabay.com/photos/city-seattle-washington-landmark-4558069/ | https://pixabay.com/photos/dessert-crepes-eat-food-gentle-5105024/ | https://pixabay.com/photos/mango-hd-mango-mango-fruit-2360551/ | https://pixabay.com/illustrations/crown-princess-prince-laurels-1174116/ | https://pixabay.com/illustrations/gold-foil-crown-tiara-crown-queen-5262245/

Meet The Royal Author

Queen Mylan Adwoa Javeen Morisseau

The author, Mylan A. J. Morisseau, shares her amazing dream of traveling around the world. Mylan's travel exploration brings joy and inspiration to her sister and nieces in a special way. This book opens the world to its readers by introducing a multitude of continents and gorgeous sites along the way.

Mylan Morisseau is 17 years old and resides in Land O Lakes, Florida. Mylan's mentor and teacher has been none other than her mother, Dr. Mavis Morisseau.

Mylan loves helping her peers at school overcome challenges in daily living and self-esteem issues. She is truly an anointed, courageous, poet, creative artist with a great love for music. Mylan spreads the love she has for people everywhere she goes.

Mylan loves life, traveling, participating in youth events, inspiring seniors at nursing facilities, and volunteering her service helping youth at a horse ranch in Dade City, Florida.

This special project was written for her family so that they can see themselves as world travelers. The sky's the limit and when we embrace our full potential in life, we can accomplish anything we set out to do. Mylan is a firm believer of this and would like everyone to take a ride and enjoy the journey. It awaits you!

www.ingramcontent.com/pod-product-compliance
Lightning Source LLC
Chambersburg PA
CBHW050850010526
44119CB00016BA/360